ISBN 1-58660-749-9

All Scripture quotations are taken from the King James Version of the Bible.

Published by Humble Creek, P.O. Box 719, Uhrichsville, Ohio 44683

Printed in China.
5 4 3 2 1

May Christ be the Center of Your Christmas

VICKIE PHELPS

HUMBLE CREEK
INSPIRATION FOR LIFE

As we celebrate this holy season, I wish for you all the love and peace that the Christ of Christmas offers. May He truly be your focus this joyful time of year.

This delightful little book provides unique and simple ideas that will help you to have a Christ-centered Christmas. When you do this, He is sure to bless you!

ONE

Keep those traditions which emphasize the birth of Christ.

Stand fast, and hold the traditions which ye have been taught, whether by word, or our epistle.

2 THESSALONIANS 2:15

TWO

Share the Christmas story with at least one stranger this Christmas.

And when they had seen it,
they made known abroad the saying
which was told them concerning this child.

LUKE 2:17

THREE

Be patient while waiting in long shopping lines.

In your patience possess ye your souls.

LUKE 21:19

FOUR

Don't shake your finger at the driver
who reached the only empty parking space before you did.

Cease from anger, and forsake wrath:
fret not thyself in any wise to do evil.

PSALM 37:8

FIVE

Speak softly to the harried clerk behind the counter.

A soft answer turneth away wrath:
but grievous words stir up anger.

PROVERBS 15:1

SIX

Volunteer to assist with the Christmas program at your church.

With good will doing service,
as to the Lord, and not to men.

EPHESIANS 6:7

SEVEN

Read the Christmas story from Luke at least once a week during the holidays.

Thy word is a lamp unto my feet, and a light unto my path.

PSALM 119:105

EIGHT

Spend time alone with God each day.

And ye shall seek me, and find me,
when ye shall search for me with all your heart.

JEREMIAH 29:13

NINE

Concentrate on the thought behind the gift, not how much you spend.

A gift is as a precious stone in the eyes of him that hath it:
whithersoever it turneth, it prospereth.

PROVERBS 17:8

TEN

Give a holiday party for those you don't know well
instead of those in your close-knit circle of friends.

Use hospitality one to another without grudging.

1 PETER 4:9

ELEVEN

Offer to address and mail Christmas cards
for your neighbors who are shut-ins.

Look not every man on his own things,
but every man also on the things of others.

PHILIPPIANS 2:4

TWELVE

Keep Christ in your heart;
don't leave Him in the manger.

My son, give me thine heart,
and let thine eyes observe my ways.

PROVERBS 23:26

THIRTEEN

Help your elderly neighbors and friends
decorate their homes for the holidays.

*They helped every one his neighbor;
and every one said to his brother,
Be of good courage.*

ISAIAH 41:6

FOURTEEN

Spend some quiet time thinking about
the blessings in your life.

*Bless the LORD, O my soul, and forget not all his benefits:
Who forgiveth all thine iniquities;
who healeth all thy diseases;
Who redeemeth thy life from destruction;
who crowneth thee with lovingkindness and tender mercies;
Who satisfieth thy mouth with good things;
so that thy youth is renewed like the eagle's.*

PSALM 103:2–5

FIFTEEN

Write a family holiday letter describing how Christ has worked in your family this year.

Every good gift and every perfect gift is from above, and cometh down from the Father of lights.

JAMES 1:17

SIXTEEN

Read Christmas stories and books that emphasize the birth of Christ.

And thou shalt teach them diligently unto thy children, and shalt talk of them when thou sittest in thine house.

DEUTERONOMY 6:7

SEVENTEEN

Play CDs or cassettes containing songs about the true meaning of Christmas.

I will sing unto the LORD as long as I live: I will sing praise to my God while I have my being.

PSALM 104:33

EIGHTEEN

Give a gift such as an extra monetary gift
to your church, a charitable foundation,
or a needy family in honor of Christ.

*Every man according as he purposeth in his heart,
so let him give; not grudgingly, or of necessity:
for God loveth a cheerful giver.*

2 Corinthians 9:7

NINETEEN

Mend a broken relationship.

*Therefore if thou bring thy gift to the altar, and there
rememberest that thy brother hath ought against thee;
Leave there thy gift before the altar, and go thy way;
first be reconciled to thy brother,
and then come and offer thy gift.*

Matthew 5:23–24

TWENTY

Give gifts that focus on Christ. Bibles, Christian books, and music or membership to a Christian organization are all good ideas.

Those things, which ye have both learned, and received, and heard, and seen in me, do: and the God of peace shall be with you.

PHILIPPIANS 4:9

TWENTY-ONE

Invite someone new to visit your church during the month of December.

LORD, I have loved the habitation of thy house, and the place where thine honour dwelleth.

PSALM 26:8

TWENTY-TWO

Open a Bible to Luke 2 and
place it in the center of your decorations.

And it came to pass in those days,
that there went out a decree from Caesar Augustus,
that all the world should be taxed.

Luke 2:1

TWENTY-THREE

Place a nativity scene in each room of your home.

And she brought forth her firstborn son,
and wrapped him in swaddling clothes,
and laid him in a manger.

Luke 2:7

TWENTY-FOUR

Take the family caroling.
Sing songs about the birth of Christ.

Make a joyful noise unto the Lord, all ye lands.

Psalm 100:1

TWENTY-FIVE

Buy and send out Christ-centered holiday cards.

Behold, I bring you good tidings of great joy.

LUKE 2:10

TWENTY-SIX

Teach your children Christmas carols
which tell the true meaning of the season.

O come, let us sing unto the LORD:
let us make a joyful noise to the rock of our salvation.

PSALM 95:1

TWENTY-SEVEN

To get another view of the Christmas story,
read it in more than one Bible version.

The heart of the prudent getteth knowledge;
and the ear of the wise seeketh knowledge.

PROVERBS 18:15

TWENTY-EIGHT

If you have small children,
have them act out the Christmas story as told in the Bible.

For unto you is born this day in the city of David
a Saviour, which is Christ the Lord.

LUKE 2:11

TWENTY-NINE

Get involved in community holiday activities,
expressing your Christian world view.

Go ye therefore, and teach all nations. . .teaching them to
observe all things whatsoever I have commanded you.

MATTHEW 28:19–20

TIIIRTY

Enter the local Christmas parade,
designing a float with a Christ-centered theme.

Let your light so shine before men,
that they may see your good works,
and glorify your Father which is in heaven.

MATTHEW 5:16

THIRTY-ONE

Plan your devotional time for December
around a study of Christ.

Study to shew thyself approved unto God,
a workman that needeth not to be ashamed,
rightly dividing the word of truth.

2 TIMOTHY 2:15

THIRTY-TWO

Trim your tree with ornaments or symbols
which point to some part of the Christmas story.
Example: Angels, stars, nativity figures.

Where is he that is born King of the Jews?
for we have seen his star in the east,
and are come to worship him.

MATTHEW 2:2

THIRTY-THREE

Bake cookies in the shapes of symbols that point to some part of the Christmas story such as angels and stars.

When they saw the star, they rejoiced with exceeding great joy.

MATTHEW 2:10

THIRTY-FOUR

Build a nativity scene for your yard
and invite neighborhood children to help set it up,
using this as an opportunity to share the story of Christ.

Thou shalt love thy neighbour as thyself.

GALATIANS 5:14

THIRTY-FIVE

Keep peace with your spouse.
Make a special effort to show him or her love
during the holidays when tempers are short.

Better is a dry morsel, and quietness therewith,
than an house full of sacrifices with strife.

PROVERBS 17:1

THIRTY-SIX

Be diligent in all your financial affairs.
Don't overspend.

Moreover it is required in stewards,
that a man be found faithful.

1 CORINTHIANS 4:2

THIRTY-SEVEN

Don't allow yourself to get caught up in
a shopping frenzy over certain popular trends.

Set your affection on things above,
not on things on the earth.

COLOSSIANS 3:2

THIRTY-EIGHT

While waiting in the supermarket checkout line,
allow someone with fewer purchases to go ahead of you.

Therefore all things whatsoever ye would that men should do to
you, do ye even so to them.

MATTHEW 7:12

THIRTY-NINE

Offer to help an elderly friend or neighbor with his or her holiday shopping.

As we have therefore opportunity, let us do good unto all men.

Galatians 6:10

FORTY

Maintain quality family time during the hectic season.

She looketh well to the ways of her household, and eateth not the bread of idleness.

Proverbs 31:27

FORTY-ONE

Wrap your gifts in religious-themed paper.

The gift of God is eternal life through Jesus Christ our Lord.

Romans 6:23

FORTY-TWO

Determine to give the word "peace" new meaning in your life.

Depart from evil, and do good; seek peace, and pursue it.

PSALM 34:14

FORTY-THREE

Do your own research into the meaning of the gifts the wise men brought to the stable.

And when they had opened their treasures,
they presented unto him gifts;
gold, and frankincense, and myrrh.

MATTHEW 2:11

FORTY-FOUR

Offer to help a busy friend clean her house during the holiday season.

[She] worketh willingly with her hands.

PROVERBS 31:13

FORTY-FIVE

Give a gift to someone and sign the card, "In Jesus' name."

And whatsoever ye do in word or deed,
do all in the name of the Lord
Jesus, giving thanks to God and the Father by him.

COLOSSIANS 3:17

FORTY-SIX

Choose a secret pal for yourself,
and send him or her a note or card with a
scripture verse each week during December.

And be ye kind one to another.

EPHESIANS 4:32

FORTY-SEVEN

Buy some inexpensive Bibles and
give them to a mission or children's home.

Heaven and earth shall pass away:
but my words shall not pass away.

MARK 13:31

FORTY-EIGHT

Adopt a needy family during the holidays and do something special for them each week in December.

Verily I say unto you, Inasmuch as ye have done it unto one of the least of these my brethren, ye have done it unto me.

MATTHEW 25:40

FORTY-NINE

Take time to listen to someone in need.

Blessed are the merciful: for they shall obtain mercy.

MATTHEW 5:7

FIFTY

Write a letter to the editor of your local paper complimenting the businesses who decorate with spiritual Christmas themes.

Ye are the light of the world.
A city that is set on an hill cannot be hid.

MATTHEW 5:14

FIFTY-ONE

Watch the words you speak during this time of the year.
Speak words of peace.

Only let your conversation be as it becometh the gospel of Christ.

PHILIPPIANS 1:27

FIFTY-TWO

Endeavor to stay calm in the midst of all the frenzy.

For God is not the author of confusion, but of peace.

1 CORINTHIANS 14:33

FIFTY-THREE

While you're driving during the busy holiday season, remember that the Christ of Christmas is one of your passengers.

And whatsoever ye do, do it heartily, as to the Lord, and not unto men.

COLOSSIANS 3:23

FIFTY-FOUR

Allow extra time for traveling to worship services so you won't be rushed and will arrive fresh and relaxed.

This is the day which the LORD hath made;
we will rejoice and be glad in it.

PSALM 118:24

FIFTY-FIVE

Be courteous to other drivers.
Allow them into traffic lanes ahead of you.

I can do all things through Christ which strengtheneth me.

PHILIPPIANS 4:13

FIFTY-SIX

Renew your commitment to Christ during the season.

And be not conformed to this world:
but be ye transformed by the renewing of your mind.

ROMANS 12:2

FIFTY-SEVEN

Share at least one meal a day with the entire family. Schedule activities so they don't interfere with mealtimes.

She riseth also while it is yet night, and giveth meat to her household, and a portion to her maidens.

Proverbs 31:15

FIFTY-EIGHT

Ask a different family member to say grace at each meal, and to give thanks for what Christmas means to them.

Giving thanks always for all things unto God and the Father in the name of our Lord Jesus Christ.

Ephesians 5:20

FIFTY-NINE

Bake cookies for your mail carrier, hairdresser, or other service workers. Attach a printed copy of the Christmas story.

He that giveth, let him do it with simplicity. . . with cheerfulness.

Romans 12:8

SIXTY

Send an appreciation card to your minister.

Let brotherly love continue.

HEBREWS 13:1

SIXTY-ONE

While wrapping gifts,
pray for the individual who is receiving each gift.

*Now therefore let it please thee to bless the house of thy servant,
that it may be before thee for ever:
for thou blessest, O LORD, and it shall be blessed for ever.*

1 CHRONICLES 17:27

SIXTY-TWO

After addressing your Christmas cards,
pray over the stack of cards,
asking God's blessing on each individual.

The effectual fervent prayer of a righteous man availeth much.

JAMES 5:16

SIXTY-THREE

Keep a journal during the season.
Write favorite Bible verses and list the blessings
that come your way each day.

Bless the L*ORD*, *O my soul, and forget not all his benefits.*

PSALM 103:2

SIXTY-FOUR

Refrain from making negative statements
such as "bah humbug" about Christmas.

Let no corrupt communication proceed out of your mouth,
but that which is good to the use of edifying,
that it may minister grace unto the hearers.

EPHESIANS 4:29

SIXTY-FIVE

Share a smile with everyone you meet
whether they return it or not.

Beloved, let us love one another: for love is of God.

1 JOHN 4:7

SIXTY-SIX

Obtain a Middle East map or Bible map for your children. Using a magic marker, trace Joseph and Mary's journey to Bethlehem and relate the story as you trace.

And Joseph also went up from Galilee, out of the city of Nazareth, into Judaea, unto the city of David, which is called Bethlehem.

LUKE 2:4

SIXTY-SEVEN

Visit a local nursing home. If possible, gather the residents in a community room and read the Christmas story aloud, sing carols, and invite some of the residents to share Christmas memories.

Knowing that whatsoever good thing any man doeth, the same shall he receive of the Lord, whether he be bond or free.

EPHESIANS 6:8

SIXTY-EIGHT

Donate some clothes to a local homeless shelter
or Goodwill center.

She stretcheth out her hand to the poor;
yea, she reacheth forth her hands to the needy.

PROVERBS 31:20

SIXTY-NINE

Decorate a small tree with Christian symbols and take it to
a local orphanage, homeless shelter, or mission.

My little children, let us not love in word, neither in tongue;
but in deed and in truth.

1 JOHN 3:18

SEVENTY

Set aside time during the season
to pray for your community.

Pray without ceasing.

1 THESSALONIANS 5:17

SEVENTY-ONE

Put a verse from Luke 2 on your answering machine.

Glory to God in the highest,
and on earth peace, good will toward men.

LUKE 2:14

SEVENTY-TWO

Resist the holiday blues.

Thou wilt keep him in perfect peace,
whose mind is stayed on thee:
because he trusteth in thee.

ISAIAH 26:3

SEVENTY-THREE

Don't be rude to telephone solicitors.

Let every man be swift to hear,
slow to speak, slow to wrath.

JAMES 1:19

SEVENTY-FOUR

Call your parents just to say, "I love you."

Honour thy father and mother;
which is the first commandment with promise;
That it may be well with thee,
and thou mayest live long on the earth.

EPHESIANS 6:2–3

SEVENTY-FIVE

Have a heart-to-heart talk with your children about giving at Christmas.

Train up a child in the way he should go:
and when he is old, he will not depart from it.

PROVERBS 22:6

SEVENTY-SIX

At mealtime, have your family sing a Christmas carol together.

Sing unto the LORD, bless his name;
shew forth his salvation from day to day.

PSALM 96:2

SEVENTY-SEVEN

Donate some non-perishable food items to a local food pantry.

Blessed is he that considereth the poor: the LORD will deliver him in time of trouble.

PSALM 41:1

SEVENTY-EIGHT

Do a spiritual checkup during the holiday season.

Examine yourselves, whether ye be in the faith.

2 CORINTHIANS 13:5

SEVENTY-NINE

Be especially considerate of elderly people.

Be kindly affectioned one to another with brotherly love; in honour preferring one another.

ROMANS 12:10

EIGHTY

Keep your mind centered on Christ
instead of commercial trappings.

For where your treasure is, there will your heart be also.

MATTHEW 6:21

EIGHTY-ONE

Don't become overwhelmed by trying
to have a perfect holiday.

Rest in the LORD, and wait patiently for him:
fret not thyself because of him who prospereth in his way.

PSALM 37:7

EIGHTY-TWO

Don't feel you must keep up with
anyone else's spending habits or decorating ideas.

Better is a little with righteousness than
great revenues without right.

PROVERBS 16:8

EIGHTY-THREE

Dwell on pleasant thoughts.

Finally, brethren, whatsoever things are true,
whatsoever things are honest, whatsoever things are just,
whatsoever things are pure, whatsoever things are lovely,
whatsoever things are of good report;
if there be any virtue, and if there be any praise,
think on these things.

PHILIPPIANS 4:8

EIGHTY-FOUR

Spend some time with friends you haven't seen in awhile.

A man that hath friends must shew himself friendly.

PROVERBS 18:24

EIGHTY-FIVE

Teach your children the importance of goodness.

He that handleth a matter wisely shall find good:
and whoso trusteth in the LORD, happy is he.

PROVERBS 16:20

EIGHTY-SIX

Listen to the Bible on cassette
while you clean and bake.

O how love I thy law!
It is my meditation all the day.

PSALM 119:97

EIGHTY-SEVEN

Give gift subscriptions to a Christian magazine.

The entrance of thy words giveth light.

PSALM 119:130

EIGHTY-EIGHT

Attend a community Christmas service.

Enter into his gates with thanksgiving,
and into his courts with praise.

PSALM 100:4

EIGHTY-NINE

Form a caroling group and pass out copies of Luke 2 at each home.

And all they that heard it wondered at those things which were told them by the shepherds.

LUKE 2:18

NINETY

Volunteer to babysit for a friend so she can shop, bake, or clean.

A friend loveth at all times.

PROVERBS 17:17

NINETY-ONE

Say "I love you" often to those around you during the holiday season.

Beloved, let us love one another: for love is of God; and every one that loveth is born of God, and knoweth God.

1 JOHN 4:7

NINETY-TWO

Pray over your gift list,
asking for guidance in your selection.

The steps of a good man are ordered by the LORD:
and he delighteth in his way.

PSALM 37:23

NINETY-THREE

Take time to notice God's winter creation.

For by him were all things created,
that are in heaven, and that are in earth. . .
all things were created by him, and for him.

COLOSSIANS 1:16

NINETY-FOUR

Create your own Christmas trivia game
using the Bible as your source.

Teach me, O LORD, the way of thy statutes;
and I shall keep it unto the end.

PSALM 119:33

NINETY-FIVE

Give of yourself, not just your money.

A good name is rather to be chosen than great riches,
and loving favour rather than silver and gold.

PROVERBS 22:1

NINETY-SIX

Make an extra effort to spread the gospel in some way.

Go ye into all the world,
and preach the gospel to every creature.

MARK 16:15

NINETY-SEVEN

Allow yourself time to dwell on God's gift
to us in the form of Jesus.

Thanks be unto God for his unspeakable gift.

2 CORINTHIANS 9:15

NINETY-EIGHT

Volunteer to decorate and
prepare your church for the holidays.

I was glad when they said unto me,
Let us go into the house of the LORD.

PSALM 122:1

NINETY-NINE

Write a letter to the editor of your local paper
to encourage others to celebrate
the Christ of Christmas.

Let the redeemed of the LORD say so,
whom he hath redeemed from the hand of the enemy.

PSALM 107:2

ONE HUNDRED

Make a video of your family singing Christmas carols,
reading the Christmas story from the Bible,
and praying together.
Send it to relatives who live
too far away to visit at Christmas.

And suddenly there was with the angel
a multitude of the heavenly host praising God.

LUKE 2:13

ONE HUNDRED AND ONE

Resolve to keep the Christ of Christmas
alive in your heart throughout the coming year,
not only in December.

Let this mind be in you,
which was also in Christ Jesus.

PHILIPPIANS 2:5